FRASER VALLEY REGIONAL LIBRARY

39083514619338

S0-CAX-443

# Great Clients

# Great Clients*

## *Why Their Advertising Is Better Than Yours

David Ullman

Figure.1

Vancouver / Berkeley

"Don't tell me how good you make it;
tell me how good it makes me when
I use it." LEO BURNETT

Copyright © 2020 by David Ullman

20 21 22 23 24   5 4 3 2 1

All rights reserved. No part of this book may be reproduced, stored
in a retrieval system, or transmitted, in any form or by any means,
without prior written consent from the publisher.

Cataloguing data are available from Library and Archives Canada
ISBN 978-1-77327-111-8 (pbk.)
ISBN 978-1-77327-113-2 (ebook)
ISBN 978-1-77327-112-5 (pdf)

Design by Jessica Sullivan

Editing by Michael Leyne
Copy editing by Peter Norman
Proofreading by Breanne MacDonald

Printed and bound in Canada by Friesens
Distributed internationally by Publishers Group West

Figure 1 Publishing Inc.
Vancouver BC Canada
www.figure1publishing.com

# Contents

# Introduction

This book is for people in business who are spending good money for bad advertising. The goal here is to help clients ensure that when they spend their money, they get truly effective advertising in return.

These days everywhere you and your customers turn, you're being advertised to. Traditional media, new media, social media, online, offline, whatever, it's loaded with advertising. The media is filled with talking heads, phony patients and gray-templed doctors, strange animation, cheesy production, mindless music, flashing prices, unreadable legal disclaimers and cop-out warnings of vile side effects, sexy promises of great vacations, incredible vehicles in places you and I will never see let alone drive in. Spend a couple of hours watching television, browsing through magazines, listening to the radio, or driving along in billboard country, and you'll see and hear what I mean.

So why is there so much bad advertising? Is it so hard to create compelling, interesting, entertaining, brand-building advertising that most agencies can't do it? Who's responsible for the 24/7 barrage of boring, silly, offensive advertising? Is there something strange going on?

Heresy: The advertising agencies aren't responsible. The people whose names appear in the advertising are responsible; they're the clients of agencies! Clients don't just pay bills. They see, discuss and approve of everything the agency does on their behalf. From concept to appearance in print, on TV, on your computer, in your mail, on a building... it's all done with the client's approval. Bad advertising comes from clients whose minds are closed—they already know what they like and what they don't like. These are clients who, by accident or design, are willing to compromise or set aside the work of advertising professionals. It's no more complex than that.

Sounds like I'm being harsh. I'm not. I see the creative bar being lowered every time I see an ad for automobile insurance, pharmaceuticals, cars, deodorants, retail, corporate, financial services, foods, restaurants—you name it! Same in all media that carry advertising.

I spent more than forty years in the Creative Departments at agencies in New York and Los Angeles. Every day I worked with all kinds of products and services from all kinds of big clients and all kinds of small clients. No matter, for me every day was an adventure in the "combat zone" (there were those who thought that *I* was the "combat zone"). Then I retired. I had become a consumer. That's when I began to really see and hear the bad stuff. And that's when I began to think about all this.

Reality: Great advertising comes from Great Clients. Clients that work hand in hand with their agency. Clients who demand advertising that crashes through the crap clutter and resonates with the human beings most likely to be interested in what the client has to say or sell.

This book is about Great Clients and how they are encouraging and inspiring their agencies to create great advertising. FYI: everything offered here is based on my own experience and situations I observed firsthand or participated in.

# 1.

# What the Hell Is Advertising, Anyway?*

**I**N THE BEGINNING...

Advertising probably began when one Neanderthal shouted to another that he had found a long pointy stick that would be great for hunting. He called it "Long Pointy Stick." Then an Ad Neanderthal came along and counseled that it needed a new name—"something really cool, like 'Spear.' And with a name like that you can sell it for at least four shells!"

While historians figure that advertising—"the act or practice of calling public attention to one's product, service, need," according to Dictionary.com—may have started in the late 1600s, advertising as we know it really got going in the 1920s. Since then the business of advertising has grown. A lot.

According to Statista, in 2018 nearly $230 billion U.S. was spent on advertising in North America. As best I can tell, there are better than seventeen thousand agencies in North America. The bottom line is that this is big business. It's an industry. And it's becoming more complex every day. Indeed, every time there's an even minor advance in communications, the business of advertising tends to expand a bit as they put that minor advance to work to help sell stuff. Advertising is an industry that expands and grows just about 24/7/365. These days, there's hardly a product or service that isn't advertised. All because somewhere, some ad person thinks, "Hmmmm, I have an idea for you..."

There are those who regard advertising as manipulative, convincing people that they should buy stuff they don't really need, things that won't improve their life. Others say that advertising helps stimulate an economy by helping to generate mass sales that keep the cost of goods and services reasonable. Either way, advertising has become an art, a science, and a source of entertainment. The most effective link between clients and their markets is advertising agencies and their clients. The difference between a Great Client and a bad client is what this book is all about.

# *What advertising can and can't do

The claim is that advertising can sell a product. Any product. Anytime. Anywhere. All it takes is a decent ad in the right publication. Or a decent commercial on the right station at the right time. Or a decent direct mail piece delivered to the right people.

Heresy: My experience leads me to conclude that advertising really doesn't "sell." I may fit the Range Rover demographic, the commercials are beautifully produced, and I see them when they interrupt the program I'm watching. But they simply don't move me to think about a test-drive.

I also see a lot of automobile insurance company advertising. They all tell me how much I'll save and all I have to do is pick up the phone and dial this number and we'll give you a free money-saving quote in minutes!

We had one client that proves my point. It was/is a "consumer direct" company. And boy did I have discussions with that client. His position was that when sales of policies were down, it was the fault of the advertising. I disagreed.

No matter how many calls the work we did produced (and we often produced record numbers of calls), the client was steadfast in his thinking. He measured the effectiveness of the advertising by the actual number of policies sold. I maintained my position. (I am sure he still thinks he was right. I know I was right.)

I believe that the advertising did exactly what it was supposed to do: get people to call! Once that call was made, it was up to the person who answered the call to *sell* the policy. If that person had just had a fight with his wife or just received a notice that he was being sued, that person would not answer the phone and express a genuine interest in helping the caller get the right policy at a money-saving price.

Back to the Range Rover example. Even if I were motivated to test-drive a Range Rover, it's the salesman at the dealership who'll sell me the car. Or not. If the advertising is successful, it will move people to take a test-drive. Frankly, I doubt watching a new model climb a massive staircase in China will move people to arrange for a test-drive. On the other hand, it may fall into the category called "brand building." And that ain't too bad.

I suppose the real point here is that the job of advertising is to move the consumer to do something—pick up the phone and call, look for products or find out where the product is sold, try a tankful of performance-improving gasoline or try that special toothpaste that'll brighten their smile.

Advertising can educate, inform, introduce, and create an impression and a climate for salesmen and women. It can make you want a beer while watching a football game, or make you hungry for a pizza, or make you want to try a nice place to dine or travel to, and so on. But close the deal? I don't think so.

# *People make one agency different from another

An advertising agency is a group of sharply focused people helping you build your business. They do what other businesses don't do, or don't do well. The agency product is specialized know-how from people with talents for writing and visualizing. As such, an agency will provide the client with all the folks in all the supporting services needed by the client in order to help their business grow: account management, media planning, buying and traffic, production (print and broadcast), and just about any kind of research and creative: copywriting, art direction, photography, television production, print production, online content . . . you name it.

Think of an agency as if it were a Ferrari. When you peek under the hood there are a lot of moving parts at work. Great Clients know what's connected to what; when they hear a weird squeaking sound, they can tell where it's coming from and what it means. And then they—and agency management—do what they can to ensure that the engine continues to run smoothly. In short: The parts of any advertising agency are its people. Men and women whose daily contributions make sure the "engine" runs smoothly and can get the client's business to where it wants to be.

# *What makes an agency client a Great Client?

When I landed with BBDO, an agency with plenty of experience with Great Clients, my first assignment was to work with the Armstrong Cork account. Now, get this: In 1918, the Armstrong Cork Company signed the Batten Company to handle its advertising. Today, Armstrong is Armstrong Worldwide Industries, and the Batten Company is known as BBDO. Armstrong is still their client. These guys are doing something right!

In retrospect I can honestly say that every client I worked with received nothing less than pro service and work we honestly believed would help them reach their goals. But it seemed that the work with an extra spark or two of creativity was done for clients that actually made us part of their team and appreciated the efforts being made on their behalf.

Shortly after I joined BBDO/NY, the fellow who had been handling the creative work for Remington Arms retired. I was asked if I could work with a sporting firearms account. I said, "Let me go talk with them."

So I trekked up to Remington headquarters in Bridgeport, Connecticut, and spent the day with the Advertising Director and the Advertising Manager. At the end of the day they asked if I'd be comfortable working with them and the products. I answered "Yes... with a proviso." I told them I wouldn't use pictures of guys posing with animals they'd killed, and we wouldn't write copy about what happens when a bullet hits an animal. "I will do everything I can to sell the product on its merits," I said. They were OK with that.

Back in my office, thanks to BBDO's Research Department, I began a deep dive into sporting firearms, the market and consumer profiles. There was a huge amount of research available to me, but a few really salient points began to surface. For instance, most buyers spent a significant amount of time deciding which rifle or shotgun to buy. In those days, most rifles and shotguns were sold through the big chain discount sporting goods stores, and hunters had trouble getting the information they needed about the products that interested them most.

Then my small group took a long look at the competition. Remington didn't want to compete with the low-price manufacturers, or, at the other end of the market, the custom-made or limited-production companies. That narrowed down the competition to a few significant names, which traded on their tradition and imagery: Winchester was all about cowboys. Ithaca sold a New England image. Mossberg was selling special features, bolstered on occasion by an endorsement from actor Robert Stack (a champion trap and skeet shooter). I noticed that most of the ads were in full color but were light on copy. Like they didn't have much to say about their products.

The advertising budget wasn't very big, but I had an idea I thought could work. I talked to the media guys at the agency, and they set up meetings with the outdoor and hunting-specific magazines to go over reader profiles, buying habits, etc. After that we began actual creative development work on what I thought could be a sensational campaign. We'd have to break a few conventions, write a whole lot of copy and work on a layout format that presented Remington as the premier authority in its field.

The concept was based on a simple need: hunters of all kinds and target shooters had trouble getting the information they needed to become better sportsmen and women. Remington would make sure they got it. We'd drop all the full-color two-page ads and develop a campaign based on single black and white pages. (We'd get twice the number of ad pages just by eliminating the high cost of color and the quality control it required.) With that plan in mind, I sat down with an Art Director and we created the campaign for "REMINGTON REPORTS. Information straight from the experts and engineers who design and make Remington rifles and shotguns." We were now in the business of advertising information to markets filled with prospects hungry for it.

Topping off the creative was our media strategy. To make a major impression every single month, I wanted to buy the first two pages in every publication we decided to advertise in. The response to this was terrific. Most of the time the publications gave us what we wanted. Now all that we needed to do was make the presentation to Remington's senior management. Back to Bridgeport we went. At the meeting, I explained everything in moderate detail. We spent a bit of time describing the basic concept. We showed a bunch of layouts and copy that was ready for approval to produce. They really liked the campaign, but the Marketing guys were a bit skeptical about the dotted line that ran along the bound edge of each magazine; a line that said "Cut here to save this Remington Report." I explained that every ad closed with the same offer: if a reader wants to save the report, just write us and we'll send you a folder to keep the reports in, along with the current Remington catalog. It wasn't a big hit with the Marketing guys, but the Advertising Director said something about "breaking a rule every now and then" and gave us approval to move forward as quickly as possible to gather information and get ads done and produced. He also assured us that Remington would cooperate with us fully.

The folks at Remington opened all the doors. We interviewed all sorts of skilled people who designed, engineered and manufactured Remington rifles and shotguns. And did we ever get information. Each B&W page was filled with copy, diagrams and inset photos. The look was classy and easy to read. It made the impression we wanted to make: that Remington was indeed the preeminent manufacturer of American sporting firearms.

February publications are pretty much directed to fishermen. But, unknown to me, my Remington folks tested a

Remington Reports ad in February issues of *Field & Stream* and *Outdoor Life*. I was miffed when they told me what they had done. The response, however, made me very happy. It was overwhelmingly positive—so many readers wrote in that they went through almost the entire first printing of the catalog, which they were now going to reprint.

In the first year, Remington reprinted the catalog four times. At the consumer sporting goods shows, the guys at the Remington display were constantly being asked for reprints of the Reports their readers didn't have. Reprints and folders were now part of a budget. We wrote Reports for Remington books, older products, new products—whatever it was we thought hunters and target shooters would be interested in. Remington awareness went way up. Sales too.

I now had a "process" that stayed with me throughout my career. Equally important as my efforts was the client side of the equation. The Remington people treated me, us, with respect from the start. When corporate meetings were about things likely to affect the advertising, I was invited to participate. I became part of the Remington organization. The work we did was never dismissed out of hand. If we went off base, they helped us get back on the right track. Approvals were prompt and complete.

They may not have exemplified every single Great Client practice suggested here, but the attitude and professionalism that helped me through my career began with the Remington people. In retrospect, they were my first Great Client.

# *What makes
an agency client
a bad client?

It's easy to be a bad client. In fact, I'd be willing to bet that most bad clients aren't aware that they're bad clients.

In the advertising business, "bad" is usually an attitude. It's an attitude that comes from the idea that the client/agency relationship is basically adversarial. After all, these clients regard their agency as a "vendor"; an expense that, most often, is charged to Sales. Not a good sign.

A bad client brings his or her personal point of view—which will eventually become adversarial in nature—to bear on the agency/client relationship. They are more interested in what they think the advertising should be than what the agency thinks. They know exactly how the commercial should go, what the print ads should look like, how the copy for everything should be written. They know how to improve upon just about everything the agency does. When asked why they reject what the agency presents, they respond with something like "I don't know. I just don't like it." That's really helpful. Or "Well, I showed the ad to my wife, and she didn't like the layout. I mean, she studied design in high school."

Many bad clients don't watch much television or even listen to the radio, except maybe in their car. They may read a magazine or check out billboards. They also have an attitude built around the fact that they are paying the agency and, as such, they are the Master. In short, bad clients want the agency to back off and do what they're told. Crappy advertising is usually the result.

In one meeting, a high-tech client told me, out of the blue, how much he had spent with the agency so far. He wanted to know how he could reduce that number. I answered, "That's easy. Give us less to do." He didn't think I was at all amusing.

A simple truth: when you're working on a lucrative account with a major client, it's natural to fall into the mindset of "the customer is always right." Even if clients plainly don't know what the hell they're doing, they're treated with deference and patience. Because without their fees, the agency employees could be out on their asses. So the agency continues to roll over until, finally, the client moves to another agency because "those guys just didn't get it." And consumers continued to be bored.

When the advertising is awful, when it doesn't work, far too often the agency is taken to task. The simple truth is that in the end an agency will, can, only do what the client wants it to do. Bad advertising comes from bad clients. It's no more complex than that!

As I see it, there is no shortage of talented, professional creative thinkers and doers: Copywriters, Art Directors, photographers, commercial producers and directors, etc. But there is a definite shortage of Great Clients.

# 2

# What's So Special About Advertising Agencies?*

**A**GENCY PEOPLE AREN'T EXACTLY your average white-collar workers. In my experience, agency folks can get a little crazy, arrogant, political . . . they take lunches that are longer than the usual, they get angry and loud. I've even seen a punch or two thrown. On average, working in an agency is (putting it politely) really intense.

It isn't glamorous. The days can be long, the nights even longer. Weekends are often given up to meet deadlines or solve problems. Going way beyond a job description to make sure a new business presentation goes off without a hitch is normal. Having to sit across the table from a client who is rejecting work but unable to explain why is frustrating as hell. Being told not to take rejection personally is demoralizing because advertising people do take it personally. Frankly, every day most advertising people spend more time thinking about a client's business than they do about anything else. The professionals in a Creative Department put their butts on the line every day. After all, if the work doesn't work for the client, they could be out a job. Same with account people . . . if an Account Executive fails to provide the right level of knowledge and service, he or she will be revising their resume. And if the agency loses a big client, everyone involved has a job that's on the line. But when all is said and done, you won't find a group of people more ready, willing and able to come out of the gate and get their job done as best as they can. Every time.

On a day-to-day basis, the Great Clients are very much aware of the people at their agency. They know who the Creative Director is and what he or she thinks about the world of good and bad advertising. They understand that the pressures on the CD are enormous. The CD is, after all, the one responsible for the agency's most visible products: the TV and radio commercials, billboards, brochures, direct mail pieces, magazine and newspaper ads, social media and digital advertising.

Account Executives manage everything involved with the relationship between the agency and its clients. Media Planners and Buyers really have to be well versed about what's happening in virtually every market of interest to the clients. Copywriters and Art Directors are continually searching for ideas and then confronting the blank screen every day. It's all hard and demanding work. Deadlines are the rule. Most advertising people never get rich. But they really enjoy the work and the people they're working with ... and they're happy to go the extra mile for most clients. They are pros.

# *Advertising agencies aren't your typical business-school business

Like any business, an advertising agency is in business to make money, to build profits. Were you to get a look at a schematic diagram of an average-sized ad agency, you'd conclude that an agency is a lot like other average-sized businesses. You'd see leadership at the top, a CEO, CFO, COO, and below that the leadership folks, directors, managers and all sorts of other functionaries with titles, until at the very bottom of the diagram are the people actually doing the work to make the products to be sold. Pretty standard stuff.

But appearances can be misleading. While an agency may have a chart showing the agency's structure, that chart may be short-lived depending on the size of the agency and how it might look when it reaches a certain growth level. On the other hand, there may not be a chart.

An agency can kind of plan for growth, but it really can't accurately predict when that growth will occur. Or where that growth will come from. Put simply, an agency is a business predicated on opportunity. One day the agency may be struggling to meet its payroll, and the next they've landed a client that can take their business beyond expectations. Despite what the guys with an MBA from Harvard may tell you, acquiring new clients is tough, unpredictable, and it's foolish to bank on successful new business development programs.

At the heart of most agencies will be a mix of people assuming responsibilities for certain basic agency functions. These people will offer differing backgrounds and disciplines. What they may have in common is the understanding that an advertising agency is a service organization. It's that simple.

I know a gentleman with a law degree who made his mark starting out as a Copywriter and from there became a senior creative executive at a very large international agency. I knew an Art Director who made an excellent living despite having no art skills at all. Stick figures were his thing. But he could visualize with exceptional clarity and relevance. I once had a creative colleague whose claim to fame was that he had been a game show host! A successful Account Executive usually has a background in a business close to the business the client is in.

Agencies simply do not fit into a mold. A four-man "shop" may be making money hand over fist with just one client while a large agency struggles to find clients that won't conflict with the clients already on their client roster. And other agencies may have several clients with similar budgets. That approach may provide a solid financial base, but the agency may still be looking for the breakthrough client that agency reputations are built on. And advertising agencies come in several sizes.

"Small" could be an Art Director and a Copywriter sharing a small office. Billing is probably in the neighborhood of "enough to live on." They rely on outsourcing tasks like media planning, buying and tracking, research and video production. Low cost for inside services. Creative is likely to be OK.

"Medium" is a step up. A small staff of folks with enough experience to enable a few people to handle more than one job... their own. They have some billings, up to fifteen million. They use freelancers to increase their production, research and media capabilities. The term usually applied is "boutique agency." Cute. As such, it costs a bit more than expected. Creative can be pretty good.

"Large" is a big jump. They can claim upwards of twenty-five million in billings (if you convert the actual amount of sales to the old commission rate of 15 percent). They have a dozen or so people on staff. Nobody's getting rich, but the work gets done. The clients are happy. They often rely on outsourcing to meet special needs and reduce lengthy time-tables in order to meet client deadlines. Costs more, but you get more; people with more experience, talent and know-how. Creative work will be nothing less than "really good" if allowed to be.

"Extra-large" agencies have real departments staffed with an appropriate number of experienced people. The top people are making good money. The clients are kept happy with knowledgeable Account Executives and responsive creative. Agencies at this level know what they're doing and constantly look for new clients for growth. Each department, when needed, will use outside people to handle big projects. Creative talent usually is very good when clients allow.

"Jumbo" are the truly big guns in the advertising business. They have plenty of people to cover all salient departments for big clients. Their biggest problem is finding new clients that don't conflict with their existing clients. The agencies often grow by buying smaller agencies with a decent client list. These guys are national and international. There's nothing they can't get done. Money doesn't really count when outside resources are required. What counts is keeping their clients happy and in the fold. Cost will be higher, and so will the quality of the creative work, which will be first class if permitted.

This section began with a statement about agencies not fitting a mold. That's a simple truth. However, the "definitions" offered here are not intended to represent standards. Which is to say that the variations are legion. At one time, a "large" agency in Los Angeles (Carson/Roberts) had one client: a large, international automobile manufacturer. One day the client left. The next day the agency closed its doors. And that was that. Sometimes the agency business can be rough.

# *Advertising shouldn't be a subset of Marketing or Sales

Marketing. Advertising. Sales. Three different functions. Each linked to the other, each requiring people from different places with different professional skill sets and talents.

More heresy! After quite a bit of thought and analysis of my experience, I have to say advertising simply does not belong under the wing of the Marketing or Sales Department. Yet somehow Advertising ends up having to report to or get approval from those departments.

I am fully aware that this may label me as narrow-minded, as another arrogant "creative type," or as someone who doesn't play well with others. The problem I have is that Marketing is as different from Advertising as Advertising is different from Sales! Marketing people are different than Advertising people, as are Advertising people from Sales people.

Great advertising is the product of sharply focused thinking, meaningful concepts and effective copywriting, art direction and execution. I've not seen a Marketing person visualize and create a stand-apart layout or TV storyboard. I've never read a piece of copy from salespeople that convinced a reader that a product was worth trying. I've never seen a Marketing person stand up in a room full of distributors and reps and make a presentation that kept them awake.

There was a time when a Y&R client I worked with (a winery) told us that their marketing group had discovered there may be a market for grappa (a type of clear Italian brandy made from what's left after wine grapes have been pressed). The Marketing guys prepared a program to test the feasibility of the product, which included trial sales through distribution in various parts of the country. They analyzed the demographics of the potential customer. And they developed what amounted to creative approaches for print advertising. The message they decided would best reach the consumer was that grappa could be enjoyed by anyone at any time.

Sales through distribution? Mass market consumer profiles? Creative approaches for the product's launch using print media? Hmmmm.

The client's own research indicated that there might be an opportunity for grappa but offered little of value on what that opportunity might look like. But our studies led us to conclude that its reputation for use as a cocktail would help to build high consumer interest quickly. We based our launch approach on that piece of information. Our tactic was to treat every ad as if it were a billboard.

We presented an advertising launch campaign predicated on a single line. The visual was a glistening pour of grappa and one line: "Introducing the First Real Threat to Vodka in 30 years."

The layouts were quickly reviewed and all but the Marketing folks were pleased. The Sales guys were happy because it gave them something new to crow about. Marketing guys insisted we include copy that described flavor. I won that argument. The Chairman thought "Threat" was "like a punch in the nose." He offered "Challenge." I countered that "Threat" would score higher readership than the overused "Challenge." Lost that one.

We got our approvals, but a couple of days later the effort was stopped. The client decided that they weren't going to produce grappa. It happens.

The point? Marketing did its thing and handed the project off to us. We did our thing and were ready to provide the distribution channel guys with something special for them to take into the field with a pre launch promotion. The distribution would start the chatter about a new product! It's a shame we didn't get a chance to prove it. But the process illustrates how Marketing, Advertising and Sales should represent a horizontal line rather than a vertical line on an organizational chart.

There was a time when this was the default: the Marketing Director led a group whose job was to define the business opportunity, the Director of Sales set quotas and did what was needed to move product from a warehouse to retail shelves and to consumers, and the Advertising Director made sure the agency was on the right track. All three directors and their staff worked alongside each other, and all three had the same mission: help make sure the client's company grows.

I can't tell you when those three functions were collapsed and became the Marketing Director's responsibility, and I won't speculate as to why it happened. None of that is important. What is important is that ignoring the differences between these three distinctively different functions—not to mention the corporate fetish for consensus—leads to bad advertising.

At the root of my point of view is the idea that Account Executives, researchers, Media Planners and Buyers, etc. are really important but agency creative is supported by all those functions. In turn, it's creative that reflects the accuracy of Marketing and generates impact to support Sales. It's that simple.

# *The heart of the agency is the Creative Department

The real difference between one agency and another is its "creative product." Great Clients understand that the Creative Department is where all the marketing data, consumer studies and sales strategies become grist for the mills of Copywriters, Art Directors, Creative Directors, Storyboard Artists and others ... all contributing to the effort.

It's where ideas and concepts are developed and come to life. This is where what the consumers will hear, read and watch is created and built. It's where a layout becomes a print ad, a brochure or a postcard. It's also a place where tempers can rise, sparks can fly, laughing is out loud and there are times when the language is ... colorful.

The professional men and women in the Creative Department are not management types. They're not accountants. They're not salesmen or women. In fact, most of the time, no matter where they are, their brains aren't far from what they do for a living. They know that they never know when a "Eureka!" moment will arise. That's the moment that makes them impatient to get back to the agency.

In the Creative Department, a Copywriter and Art Director will team up to develop the words and pictures that ultimately end up out there in the consumer's world. Creatives enjoy the challenges and they enjoy the work they do as individuals. When a big project lands, a group of teams will get the process moving forward. The dialogue between teams or a pair is always wide-ranging until a thought worthy of additional investigation appears. Imagine a eureka moment every hour or so. Then the easy part begins. Copywriters sling words until they get it right. Art Directors visualize and sketch until it's where they believe it should be. "Where it should be" could mean early departure from the office or a long night of brainstorming. Creatives watch deadlines, not the clock. And it is never boring. Never. It's like that whether the agency is small, medium, large, extra-large or jumbo.

Great Clients understand that "creating" takes, more often than not, an extraordinary combination of sharp focus and mental freedom. The professionals make it look easy.

# 3.

# What Do Great Clients Want?*

**A**T THE START OF MY career, I espoused a simple creative philosophy: in a world full of color I'll go black and white; in a black and white world I'll go full color. My goal was to create advertising that would stand out from the clutter. It worked. But after a couple of years, I had a hunch that my philosophy was a bit shallow.

Then I met my first real Great Client, the Advertising Director at Remington. We talked over lunch and learned we shared philosophies. Then I had a small "aha" moment. From then on, agency and client were on precisely the same wavelength. Our philosophy, our mission for everything we did, was clear:

GAIN AND MAINTAIN HIGH LEVELS
OF POSITIVE AWARENESS IN THE MINDS OF
THE PEOPLE WE WANTED TO REACH.

Since then, through all the meetings I attended, all the stuff I listened to, all the copywriting I did, I found myself asking, "Is all this going to help build and maintain lasting market awareness for my client?"

Think of it this way: before a customer becomes a customer, let alone an evangelist for your product, they need to know it exists and what it can do for them.

For sure, you need information to develop a sharply focused understanding of the folks in your market, you need to develop and shape how the market perceives you and your products and/or services. It goes on and on. And it's all for nothing unless you generate awareness—a solid presence—in the marketplace. In some places it's called "building a brand."

# *Great Clients want to reach the Prime Prospect

Understand the "who" you need to reach and you'll be better able to evaluate the creative product. And everything else that's related to it.

In an advertising agency, every Copywriter and Art Director (the stalwarts of any creative group) will have his or her personal "creative process." The basic "process" is simply thinking. Gathering information and thinking about it, then converting thoughts into words and images. (Too simple? Well, if a way of thinking gets a Copywriter or Art Director to a concept they can work with, that's what counts.) And that process starts with identifying the target audience, or Prime Prospect.

I won't take credit for what follows, but I will tell you that these four guide points help Great Clients more effectively evaluate the creative work. This is key to what's inside the head of a Copywriter or Art Director as they start "creating."

1. **THE PRIME PROSPECT**: The person most likely to buy your product, service or company. "Most likely" is the operative phrase here. Developing a profile from a bulk number of people sharing basic demographics, in a specific geographical area, isn't good enough. For example, if you make really good, somewhat pricey fishing rods, you need to know how many avid fishermen there are in the area. It's the avid fisherman who'll spend his money with you. Not the guy teaching his six-year-old to ride a two-wheeler. Simple, right?

2. **THE PRIME PROSPECT'S PROBLEMS**: You need to know what confronts your Prime Prospect every business and personal day. This could also be called a "Psychographic Profile." Do they have hobbies or personal interests? If they have a family, what about their kids? What is their financial or social position likely to be? Are they professionally on their way up, holding their own or worried about keeping their job? Where do they vacation?

Ask yourself: Does the creative communicate that you fully understand what the Prime Prospect has to deal with every day?

3. **THE SOLUTION TO THE PRIME PROSPECT'S PROBLEMS**: In today's world, whatever's unique doesn't stay that way for long. It's increasingly difficult to find those compelling reasons to buy. They exist, however, and you'll find them in a place called "knowing your customer." If you've spent enough time on the above points, have drilled down deep, way past

price and standard demographics into understanding what your customers deal with every day, then you'll be able to make a compelling case for your product or service. With a thorough understanding of the Prime Prospect and their problems, the solution just about presents itself.

Ask yourself: Does the creative effectively present how the product or service will fit into the Prime Prospect's life and solve their "problems"?

**4. CRASH THROUGH THE CLUTTER:** Media guys love to talk about "impressions." A commercial on a TV delivers a zillion impressions. A million cars pass a billboard location every day, and that converts to even more impressions. An ad in a popular article at Wired.com delivers hundreds of thousands of impressions in a single week. That said, the advertising clutter is massive. Our twenty-first-century brain has built walls that allow only those messages that resonate to get into your mind. If my client is a maker of niche computers, that's relatively easy. On the other hand, selling a flavor is something else!

I once pitched a client who was really unhappy with his advertising. The conversation was pretty routine until he asked what a "compelling reason to buy" was. Rather than answer directly, I decided to demonstrate the point. I asked him what his great passion was. The answer? Corvettes. And seeing how he was young, articulate, bright and good looking, I asked about his personal life. He told me he greatly enjoyed dating: dinners out, theater, concerts. Then I bet him fifty dollars that I could write a headline and full page of copy that would compel him to read every single word and then call the number at the end of the ad for a free brochure.

He bit. I went to the whiteboard, grabbed a marker and wrote:

HOW TO USE A CORVETTE
TO MEET MORE GIRLS!

He paid up.

It wasn't that the headline was "creative." It wasn't that I was brilliant. But by asking two simple personal questions, I got enough information to write a very simple headline that would crash through the advertising clutter and resonate inside his ad-numbed brain.

Ask yourself: Does this creative carry a message that'll resonate with the Prime Prospect? And resonating with the Prime Prospect is Job #1 in advertising.

I would guess that just about every decent agency in the country uses points like this in some way or another. But if there's a difference between me and the next guy, this is it: I put identification of the Prime Prospect and the understanding of the Prime Prospect in the first two spots because I want to understand a client's product or services from the Prime Prospect's point of view. I can't tell you how many times I've heard an ad guy say to a new or prospective client, "Tell me about your product . . ." This is usually where I interrupt: "First, tell me about the person most likely to buy your product."

# *Great Clients know who their real competition is

Once you've zeroed in on that Prime Prospect, the agency can begin to develop advertising with impact, and the media folks can plan on how best to reach those people. To do that, you need to understand the competition your advertising faces... and it's not who you think it is.

For the moment, let's suppose there's a small computer company called PalTech. PalTech has decided to market its computer systems and special software to small businesses across the country, region by region. Once successful in the first region, they'll move into the next, and so on. It just so happens that there are several major computer companies that also have targeted the small business owner/operator. What that means is that the competition will be tough.

There are plenty of business technology publications available. The most influential are loaded with big ads from the major companies. Most of the ads are as you might expect: lots of technology and benefits to small businesses, great pricing, finance plans available. The usual.

PalTech has resigned themselves to using these publications. They know competing against the big guys will be rugged and require some big bucks. But in this case their competition isn't just the ads from the computer companies—they are competing for readership with every other ad in the magazine. Every ad, big or small, is their competition—no matter what the ads are selling!

Too many clients don't quite understand that no matter what, how or why they're advertising, they are competing for attention from readers, viewers, listeners, people who receive mail, who drive by billboards, and on it goes. That's why it's so important to know as much as you can about the people most likely to buy what you're selling. That knowledge is where advertising that stands apart from the crowd comes from. Simple.

# *Great Clients hate to work in the dark

Great Clients avoid the dark. It's where dumb problems lurk; problems that need not arise. Nowhere is that light needed more than when it comes time to develop and execute the creative side of the advertising. A "Creative Brief" is what it takes to avoid the dark.

The value of a properly prepared Creative Brief can't be denied. This one document ensures that everyone involved fully understands the scope and nature of the assignment. It can provide criteria to be used when evaluating the creative work done by both agency and client. In fact, it can serve as a standard for all advertising and any other outgoing communications. Without a Creative Brief, there's no way to effectively and objectively evaluate or improve the creative work presented by the agency.

Everybody talks about a Creative Brief, and then they treat it like a simple recitation of information everyone involved already knows. They are wrong. To dismiss the value and purpose of the Creative Brief is to bring pure luck and personal taste into the equation. Ask questions based on the Brief, and the answers will be spot on.

Most Great Clients think that the Creative Brief should be prepared by the agency and offered to the client for review, discussion and approval. After all, it's the agency's job to deal with virtually all the tactical aspects of the client's business (e.g., media planning and buying, research). But a Creative Brief can also be prepared by the client and accepted by the agency. Either way, it will serve as a guide for all client and agency operations. It also can make sure that "being on the same page" is clearly defined.

The sample that follows is a demonstration only. The company it refers to does not exist.

DATE: January 15, 2020
CLIENT: PalTech Technology
PROJECT: Brand Launch
PREPARED BY: Aileen Callahan, Sr. Account Exec.

## 1. Client Overview

After three years of quietly selling PalTech computers to small businesses wherever they could find them, PalTech is still selling quietly. Based on highly favorable reviews in virtually all major technology periodicals, PalTech is ready to establish a brand that will separate itself from their larger, noisier competitors. PalTech is prepared to carve out and own the small business market segment. At this moment in time, PalTech's opportunities loom large provided they take a highly aggressive and focused approach to their market. They must think big to develop a new brand in an already crowded market.

## 2. The Products

PalTech computers are designed to meet the special requirements of small businesses. The PalTech "Buddy System" is Apple-like in appearance and function. It may look like a kitten but it is a Tiger in terms of performance. Each computer comes with 2 Terabytes of storage, 8 GB of RAM, and an Intel 8.7 3.6 GHz processor. To ensure maximum performance is reached easily, PalTech includes a proprietary suite of management software that makes it incredibly easy to manage a small business (accounting, loans, bills due and payable, salaries and benefits, production timetables, order management, expenses and business follow-up). Each part of the "Buddy System" is capable of handling everything for a business employing up to 49 employees.

### 3. Competitive Review

Microsoft continues to support computer makers that approach the market as a compendium of niches. They don't feel the need to specialize. Advertising is based on reaching the largest number of people using all sorts of media—TV to billboards to Direct Mail.

Microsoft is one of the two competing Kings. The other is Apple.

The Apple computer pitch is based on justifying a higher cost. New Apple buyers are impressed with the idea that the more expensive it is, the better it is. Somehow Apple has generated a user/fan base that just live and breathe Apple. TV is a major media buy and, like its products, reflects user friendliness and responsive, customer-centric service.

Behind the two Kings are plenty of smaller companies competing mostly on low prices and feature sets. While Microsoft and Apple lead the way, both companies run up against Dell Technologies from time to time.

Dell is a pretty classy act. They started out as a build-to-suit company but eventually developed a brand with some pretty jazzy features, larger screens and prices that were quite appealing. They have a line. Recent TV advertising is selling the quality, diversity and future of Dell's technology.

Overall, including TV, local advertising support and co-op advertising programs, products, Microsoft spends $1.6 billion, and while Apple no longer discloses its ad budgets, best guesses put them at better than $2 billion. TV takes the biggest chunk in each budget.

## 4. Research

Research for this market category is ongoing and plentiful. Small businesses span the entire range of goods and services, from tourism to forestry to industrial manufacturing and real estate.

In short, current research tells us that the vast number of start-ups go out of business quickly as a result of poor financing. Even with proper financing, a large number of small businesses don't make it beyond the first three years. The cause is simple: the depth of market interest in what is being offered is low. In short, prospective buyers lost interest... if they had any to begin with.

The current tech media usage trends point to digital media and television and radio. At this point, our recommendation is to hold off launching any studies until we have a firm grasp on the PalTech brand and its message. Then we can develop and plan for sharply focused studies.

If we are to create and develop a brand for PalTech, the task must be predicated on a three-year step-by-step building process. We've come to believe that a region-by-region roll-out gives PalTech a greater ability to more easily improve the campaign as it moves forward.

## 5. The "Prime Prospect"

Simple truth: small businesses are created, built and operated by individuals. Every morning they open the doors, and at the end of their very long day they lock up. Every single sale is considered a success. The goal is not necessarily to make a fortune but to stay in business another day, week or month. It's personal. And it'll stay personal no matter how large the business may grow.

On average, owners are 35 to 40 years old. They've decided that the best way for them to grow, be happy and make some money is to not work for somebody else. These people are self-confident, independent, creative, prepared to work and prepared to learn with intensity. They bring to their business a high level of enthusiasm and naivety. They know they'll make mistakes and, most of the time, are overly cautious. Most important, they maintain their vision in spite of the business problems they confront every day—although there will be days when they ask themselves, "Why am I doing this?"

Despite all the differences between them, all small business owners build barriers around them and their business. It's a tough crowd. They have to believe before they'll buy.

## 6. Advertising Objectives

A. Position PalTech as a company that fully understands the specific problems and needs of small business owners; offer solutions geared to them and their business.

B. Use media to establish and maintain high levels of PalTech awareness within the small business market segment.

C. Develop a co-op advertising program that supports the growth of small businesses that rely on PalTech computers.

D. Develop a research program to monitor/measure quarterly levels of awareness and sales to small business owners.

E. Develop a direct sales support program covering all of the above.

## 7. Media

Given the state of the client (a new name, highly competitive market, a yet-to-be determined budget, etc.), it makes sense to begin brand development by approaching the small business market on a region-by-region basis. Each region can be reached and influenced more easily than trying to enter a larger, more competitive and expensive national market; a market where the new PalTech brand is likely to be smothered by the larger, more established competitors.

The overall objective is to impact; to introduce PalTech to small business owners/operators across the nation. While the specifics of a full media plan have yet to be determined, to reach high levels of awareness, the media most likely to be used are as follows:

TELEVISION: No other media can reach more people more effectively, more intrusively, than television. Business and General News are suggested programming. Oddly, TV tends to establish credibility if the message is serious.

PRINT: General Business Publications and those directed toward small business will be reviewed.

RADIO: Usage during AM and PM drive time will be reviewed.

LOCAL OUTDOOR: To be reviewed for possible local use.

INTERNET (e.g., Google AdWords): To be reviewed.

DIGITAL MEDIA: To be reviewed.

## 8. Creative Goals

PalTech advertising has to clearly stand apart from the claims of other companies. PalTech is a company whose promise is to solve the problems of small businesses right now. And recognizing that there is a future, PalTech will help its customers get there.

Establish PalTech as a solid brand offering solid technology at unusually "practical prices."

BELIEVABILITY: This should be a campaign based on truth. No improbable claims. Simple, straightforward statements of fact and benefits (how and why).

IDENTITY: PalTech does not want to be positioned as a high-tech company. Rather, it's a people-doing-business-with-people company. Founded just a few years ago by MIT graduates, PalTech will always be regarded as small business—no matter how large it grows.

SUSTAINABILITY: This program and campaign should be planned to run for a minimum of three years from initial brand launch until a decision, to continue or change, is made.

REASON TO RESPOND: Call for an on-site demonstration, or a trial period (unique).

STYLE: Crisp… matter of fact with a touch of self-deprecating humor. Avoid all references to wealth, performance and promises of success. The sell is problem-solving right now.

TONE: Confident but not serious. Friendly, not obsequious. Knowledgeable, but not smart-ass. The Prime Prospects are living and working in the here and now.

## 9. Creative Development

With appropriate approvals, "creative" work in two major areas will begin promptly. All work will be directed to support and enhance a strong and provocative positioning statement. E.g.:

**PalTech Technology: The most powerful
small business tool since money!**

**PalTech Technology: The most powerful
small business tool since you!**

CORPORATE IDENTITY: A new logo will be designed. New communications materials will be designed (business cards, letterheads, envelopes, etc.). Logo changes will appear on an improved PalTech website. A communications "style guide" will be prepared for internal use.

TELEVISION: Storyboards developed for two :30 spots. Each spot to be editable into :10 and/or :15 versions. Primary goal is to establish PalTech as a credible company specializing in serving small business owners/operators.

RADIO: Scripts with a single strong message. Spin from TV spots. :30 max.

PRINT: Introductory full-page color ads; ongoing fractional units with a single pointed statement in each.

ONLINE: Text ads in search results; banners in ad-network platforms; targeted social media content.

COLLATERAL MATERIAL (Sales Support): New PalTech brochure (how, why, who); PowerPoint presentation (story form).

Ideally, all that information will be stated accurately with brevity and clarity, with compelling language and, if possible, in a way that'll generate thinking and questions. Speaking of questions...

When new advertising is presented, the brief's information itself can be used to more objectively evaluate the work. Just ask simple questions that begin with *how, why, can, can't, will, does this, what, have we met, does this meet, will this influence, will this stand apart...*

Creative Briefs can be changed to meet new requirements. They can be used to help define a campaign or a single print ad, radio or TV commercial, brochure, promotion, etc. No matter how it's used, I believe a properly prepared Creative Brief is strategically and tactically important. They ensure everyone involved has a legitimate feel for the folks most likely to buy what you're selling: the primary prospect/customer. They'll be looking at the information through the prospect's eyes. With that perspective, everything else of value becomes more sharply focused. Amazing.

# *Great Clients want creative and production budgets before a project starts

Great Clients demand great TV spots professionally produced, beautifully performed, exquisitely shot and brilliantly directed and edited. It's essentially the same for still photographers shooting on location in a studio. No matter, all costs need to be estimated up front.

Even Great Clients don't like budgetary surprises. A simple, businesslike process eliminates surprises. Great Clients make sure that their agency gives them estimates, complete with payment terms, for review and approval, before actual work begins. Before a lick of work is done, you need to approve estimates for the following:

· Storyboards/layouts
· Final copy complete with disclaimers
· Final selection of director or photographer
· Final selection (with director) of talent

· Final review and approval of production estimate
· Final review and approval of all schedules/deadlines

Bad clients may do the same, at first, but then they ask for extras, or derail the process by changing their minds, resulting in extra costs—and then they complain that the production is over budget.

Great Clients think things through ahead of time, but they also understand that a "Cost Estimate" is just that: a prediction of what a project is likely to cost. They don't grind and whine about cost overages that are reasonable and reflected in the final work. Most will consider approving an estimate on a "Not to Exceed" basis. In fact, in most cases, if the client doesn't show up on the stage and distract the men and women at work, the job may come in slightly lower than estimated.

The point here? When it comes to what things cost, no one likes surprises.

# *Great Clients want their agency to look ahead—far ahead

"Crash 'n' burn" assignments are a fact of life in the advertising business. Most agencies are capable of handling them effortlessly. At least, that's the way it should look to you. But from time to time, even Great Clients have to deal with genuine emergencies that, without question, could have been easily avoided. This is a simple truth.

For example, say you're a public company. You know an annual report will be needed. You know the numbers are always released for layout etc. at the last minute. That's OK. What isn't smart is putting off the planning and creative development needed to complete the report until you have the final numbers. Great Clients know how easy it is to avoid problems like this. But...

Together with their agency, Great Clients can look a year ahead and can usually see a half dozen events or projects the agency should be involved with. Development of those events should be on the schedule right now. Plan well ahead for an annual trade show booth, and you'll have the time for the agency to explore concepts, develop them and give you a real choice without incurring overtime production charges, etc.

Common sense tells you that the agency should be working on developing the next campaign (or two) while the current campaign is unfolding. Don't wait until sales/readership/viewership falls off. In the end, everyone saves money, time, hair, blood pressure... and the work you get from the agency will be better.

# *Great Clients want a proper approval process

Deadlines are important to the client and the advertising agency. Think of the relationship as if it were an hourglass with the client on one end and the agency on the other. Project input flows from the client through a pinch point and into the agency. Most likely several times back and forth for the same project. With several projects at work, without a schedule the pinch would jam up. When that happens, confusion reigns.

Schedules are important. And even more important is the approval process required to smoothly move a project through client to agency, and back again to the client, and then back to the agency for production and final release to the media.

Far too often the agency is asked to produce work without full and complete client approvals because someone is out of town, too busy or whatever. The agency should find a way to get the work to the client ... or simply wait for the client to approve the work. Even if that means a deadline will pass. Too bad. An approval process should be considered inviolate.

(Reality is, if it can, the agency will allow a client to breach the process).

More often than not, the big problem is delays in getting the proper approvals. Think about a storyboard for a TV commercial. On the agency side, the board shouldn't be presented until the following agency people have reviewed and approved the board for presentation to the client for their "Review and Correction":

· Copywriter
· Art Director
· Account Executive
· Creative Director

Usually there will be a first pass, to give the client a chance to see how the spot will work, make changes and send it back to the agency for correction or changes. The appropriate clients will review, note their corrections or changes and send it back to the agency with their signatures. And here's where clients can drive the agency nuts and in doing so increase the agency's costs, ergo their costs.

Let's say there are four people at the client who need to approve the storyboard. Four. Here's what usually happens:

Approver 1 reviews the board and sends it back to the agency for changes. The agency makes the changes and sends it back to Approver 1 ... who says OK and signs it off and passes it on to Approver 2. Approver 2 sees a correction that needs doing. Back to the agency and back to Approver 2, who says OK and shoves it up to Approver 3, who wants to change a frame so it's set in a forest instead of on a beach. Back to the agency, where the Creative Director has a fit because the schedule is getting tighter. But the change to the scene is made and the board flies back to Approver 3, who now bucks the board up to Approver 4. If all goes well... the board is approved for production. The problem is that a one-week process has now taken several weeks.

When the storyboard is delivered, the review process should move in a linear fashion: 1 makes changes and sends it to 2, who makes corrections and sends it to 3, who likes it and sends it up to 4, who would like the ending logo to be a bit larger in the frame. The key is for all changes to be made by those whose approval is needed *before* it goes back to the agency!

The agency will do whatever work is required and send the new storyboard back to the client for the approval to produce to get it done under a production start deadline that's approaching quickly.

The truth is that most storyboards, layouts, etc. go through more than one round for approval to produce. That's OK... but to get the job done by one approver at a time is silly, takes a lot of time and is maddening because waiting at the end of every approval process is a schedule deadline.

The approval process should be sleek, fast and sure. It can all start with a big rubber stamp (or the digital equivalent) with space for a date and agency and client initials. A fundamental tool for sure.

# 4

# How Great Clients Build Great Relationships*

**I**S YOUR DOCTOR A VENDOR? Do you think of your banker as a vendor? How about your attorney?

"Vendor." What a crummy word. And certainly not applicable to agency people. Self-serving? Maybe. But when you employ an advertising agency, you are not dealing with vendors. You are dealing with knowledgeable, talented professionals and specialists who will work hard to help your company become more successful. If you view these people as vendors, you will, in turn, be regarded as little more than a customer.

Most agency folks will tell you from Day 1 that they will become deeply involved with you and your company. Nice words, but that level of involvement rarely happens, mostly because lurking among some members of your staff are things like resentment ("Why do we need an agency?"), second-guessing the choice ("I preferred the other guys"), general professional insecurity ("Are they doing a better job than me?") and unhelpful feelings about advertising in general ("Advertising is just an expense, they're just vendors, why do they need to be at meetings?").

This is really about an attitude. The advertising people you've decided to bring on are, without question, your new colleagues. Make sure they're welcomed and comfortably seated at your metaphorical table, and they'll work their behinds off for you.

I'm not suggesting you have every agency guy at every meeting that has to do with your business. However, there will be two or three key/senior agency people who will be better able to help you meet goals if they're actively involved, aware of the many important decisions that need to be made and hearing firsthand why and how those decisions were made.

I also believe that the obverse is true. You are, after all, investing your money in your agency and its people. So, as odd as it may sound, you have a vested interest in how the agency is run, how well or how badly they're doing. Ask the agency, "How's your business?" They'll light up.

# *Great Clients know the key to a great relationship is mutual respect

You'd think it would be the default in any professional relationship to treat the other person with respect—but it never failed to amaze me how often my colleagues and I encountered disdain from clients. Disdain? That's the word.

I mean, you'd never change a major goal after the presentation of the campaign is made. Or take weeks out of a schedule because you have a cruise to Alaska planned. You'd never do that, right? How about delaying paying an agency invoice? How about beating up on an agency guy because you simply don't like him rather than calling the agency's CEO and asking to have him taken off your account? How about continually complaining about the agency's costs? And you and your staff wouldn't think about insulting or denigrating the creative work as it was being presented. But some time ago...

It was a Monday morning when Y&R's winery account called. The client needed to see storyboards for two of its brands. No problem. The boards were to be presented at a special meeting on Thursday. Problem. The problem was solved by hiring just about every freelance Art Director and Storyboard Artist available in Los Angeles and bringing in a bunch of Copywriters. It was quite a group. All talented, experienced professionals. Monday afternoon we met and worked straight through the night. By ten AM Tuesday we had a jillion concepts. By noon we had selected three for final copywriting and storyboard illustrations. Some people went home and the rest stayed and worked straight through until early Thursday morning. We were finished by 10:30. My portfolio was packed and I was totally prepared for my first meeting with this client. I have to tell you, I was really proud of the work we did. It was great stuff!

The presentation room was big. The client and his staff lined up on one side of the conference table. I sat opposite them, alongside my Account Executive and his assistant. After a moment of pleasantries, I pulled the concept boards out of my case. Mr. Big sat between Mr. Big 2 and Mr. Big 3. The six or seven Little People sat in descending order to the table's end. As I started talking through the first concept board, I noticed that Mr. Big 3 was engrossed in writing something on a yellow legal pad. I was on frame 2 when he interrupted. "Would you mind picking up the pace? We have to see another agency." He never looked up.

"I'm sorry, I'll move right along," I replied. With that I put all the boards back in the portfolio, snapped it closed, stood up and asked, "That fast enough for you?" I walked out of the room.

A moment later, Mr. Big 2 appeared and asked if I was

alright. I was alright. He asked if I wanted to continue the presentation. "No, perhaps another time."

Back at the office, I was greeted by the agency's President and my boss. Boss was calm; President was anything but. "What the hell are you doing!?" So we had a one-sided discussion in the lobby. Before I had a chance to explain myself, my secretary came over and told me that Mr. Big himself was on the phone. "Tell him I'll call him back." She went away, came back and said, "He wants to know if you'd finish the presentation, and when." I replied, "Tell him I can do it next Tuesday!"

I turned to the President and told him that, as a senior representative of one of the largest agencies in the world, I was not going to be treated with disdain. I also told him I refused to have this guy crap all over the work prepared by a couple of dozen writers and Art Directors, including me, working with a virtually impossible deadline. No way!

I went back the next Tuesday, Mr. Big greeted me warmly and I started all over again. Mr. Big 3 had nothing on his mind except those concept boards.

Personally and professionally, I don't like being treated with disdain. Mr. Big understood that. And I spent the next few years working on that account (an account with a terrible reputation, I might add). It became a very big and profitable account. But for me it was like being on patrol 24/7/365. So I left Y&R to start my own agency.

The overriding theme of everything in this chapter is that Great Clients respect the folks they've chosen to work on their behalf. If they didn't respect the agency and the agency people, they'd cut them loose.

# *Great Clients don't play a numbers game

These days, there's hardly a meeting where numbers don't become the most important part of the discussion, no matter what the client's business is, what the product or service is, what the creative is about and what is the best way to reach the maximum number of viewers, readers and listeners. Numbers are used as a sales tool, a reason why, the basis for a marketing effort or a measurement of efficiency.

And so on. The problem here is that far too often numbers serve to justify the cost of improving a service or product, the use of one magazine or another, running commercials in one market or another, one day-part or another.

One time I worked with a client that, among other things, designed and manufactured a fairly comprehensive line of fishing rods and reels for bass, walleye, crappie, pickerel, pike, etc. The client's Marketing guys showed up with a tape of a focus group they conducted. Based on the tape, they suggested we consider a list of publications. Their recommendations were based on the ABC-certified number of subscribers—legit numbers, for sure. Nonetheless, I voiced my concern. "The men and women in your group talk about the size of the fish they've caught in inches. They're trout fishermen. The publications you're suggesting are for them. Our audience talks about the size of a fish in terms of pounds... not inches."

I contend that savvy advertising clients know precisely who is most likely to respond to their advertising before they even start looking at media. Regardless of what the numbers may indicate.

Direct mail and direct response (TV, in this case) present clients with all sorts of numbers—statistics that support the work they're doing and the outbound communications program they've developed. I find it odd that even the most sophisticated clients often fall for the ol' "Just think about this: we see an audience of a zillion folks. If we can pull just 1 percent of that number, we're golden!"

If it were that easy, that simple, then everybody with something to offer would be doing it. In prime time.

The intent here is not to demean the statisticians who develop and provide information to the advertising agencies, media and, ultimately, agency clients. I do intend this to be cautionary. In today's world, advertising has to clearly resonate with the people most likely to respond, to buy what the advertiser has to say or sell. The more you know about these people, the more accurate and helpful your statistics will be.

# *Great Clients are accountable to their agency

If things with the agency aren't as they should be, look inside first—then, if it makes sense, talk with the agency's top management. Why? I cannot think of a single large, medium or small agency that won't promise to deliver:

· Professionalism
· Honesty and fair dealings
· Understanding of you and your business
· Energy and effort to help meet your goals
· Stand-apart advertising for all media
· Outstanding creative thinking and work
· Easy access to all agency resources
· A willingness to work within budgets and timetables
· A team of likable, knowledgeable, talented pros to
  work on your account

Here's where it gets touchy. Most agencies will do their damndest to make sure all the above is delivered. However, when things aren't going as promised, Great Clients look inside their organization before jumping on the agency. They understand that advertising agencies are particularly vulnerable. After all, every one of the points mentioned above are easily screwed up by those on the client's side of the table, those who are simply ignorant, working their own agendas or believe they know more about advertising, marketing, sales promotion and media in their market than the agency does.

Remember, the agency you pick, or the one you're already at work with, has a genuine interest in making sure that all promises are kept and that you get the work they honestly believe will help you succeed.

# *Great Clients pay attention to the creatives

Great Clients want to know and understand the creative folks at the agency. They know it's important to have the Copywriters, Art Directors, Creative Supervisors and Creative Directors on their side. They want to make their relationship personal. After all, they're the professionals that will develop the concepts that'll become words and pictures that'll ultimately become the TV spots, billboards, print ads, viral videos and charity golf tournament program ads you ask to have done.

Equally important, the work they do for you is what determines the agency's success—its style, feel, tone, attitude and track record.

At one time I was part of a "New Business Task Force" at Y&R/LA. One afternoon the team assembled for the start of a new effort for a large company in Oregon. As I read the annual report, I noted that the company was doing quite well. I flipped back to the cover and noticed a picture of the

Chairman on the first page. I knew this guy. We had fished together and swapped lies together. He was a born-and-bred Oregonian. They're somewhat different. They're very people-oriented. Very.

I brought this to the attention of our team leader after he'd finished whiteboarding his agenda. I told him my hunch was that these folks were interested primarily in creative, and they would tend to make personal decisions about people to work with.

I also mentioned that I knew the Pacific Northwest quite well and our interests would be best served if only two of us made the presentation—we didn't need the full crew of Account Executives, Research Director, et al. The fact that Y&R had an international research capability would likely be of little interest to this Portland-based company.

I was not heard. The day of the pitch arrived, and six or seven Y&R/LA guys in suits showed up in the meeting room. I wore my usual blue blazer. The client group of three arrived. The long pitch went smoothly. We were thanked, and they left for their offices and we grabbed a plane back to L.A.

That night my fishing pal called to tell me that another agency was awarded the business. They really liked our creative but didn't want to get all tied up in the big agency yarn.

It may be a bit of business arrogance on my part, but creative is really where it's at!

# *Great Clients never suffer in silence

When Great Clients have an advertising problem, they talk with their agency first (never consultants). Somehow the problems get resolved. Amazing.

Most clients claim they want to build a solid relationship with their agency, a relationship built on a strong open channel of communication. Experience, however, proves otherwise.

In fact, the minute a client becomes unhappy, a client-side someone will start talking about getting a new agency. Or they bring in a "consultant" to "help improve" the advertising. Consultants are going to spend a bit of time poking around in the "advertising area" and then recommend that the client find another agency. There's news. On the other hand...

The minute a Great Client gets unhappy with the way the advertising is working, he or she will call the agency and set up a session with the agency's key people. He or she will explain the reason for their unhappiness and ask the agency to solve the problem; to put a smile on their face again.

There's every chance that the agency will respond quickly and effectively. And the agency's respect for you and your staff will increase dramatically. After all, the agency has a vested interest in developing advertising that works hard for you. Work that produces results and keeps you smiling. When you're smiling, the agency is smiling.

Great Clients don't see the need to hire a consultant to "help with the advertising." I regard consultants as highly paid assassins. Their job is to zero in on what they believe is wrong with the advertising (which really isn't hard to do if the advertising isn't working well). The consultant puts the current agency on notice and plans for an agency review. The consultant leads the review and a new agency (a favorite of the consultant) is chosen. Then the consultant looks for more targets.

If you sense that this is a personal thing with me, I suppose it is. I've seen these folks at work and I've had to work with them. I've seen and heard these people sell a bill of goods and then begin a fairly brutal process of challenging, insulting and demoralizing the agency's management, media and creative people. And I've been lucky to have senior management ask me what I thought. I told them, they agreed and the consultant was never seen again. Toward the end of my full-time advertising career, I simply refused to work with consultants or the clients that hired them. End of rant.

I am sure there are some consultants, most often in other fields, that genuinely approach their consulting as an expansion of the client's tool box. They are not destructive. They have my respect. The other guys ... don't ask.

# *Great Clients get rid of anything that screws up their agency relationship

At best, the agency/client relationship is difficult. There are plenty of sources of friction: Goal pressures. Budget pressures. Tight schedules. Differences of opinion. Personal agendas. Arrogant executives. Disdainful managers. Executives who avoid responsibility. Lengthy decision-making processes. Flabby approval processes. This is what confronts even the Great Clients every day.

It also happens that the people at the agency you chose confront the same crap from their management. When you first started working with the agency, everyone talked about the importance of teamwork and pushing for the best work, and how important the agency's efforts are to the success of the company. There's every chance they meant it all. Then...

You left the room and the rats took over and told the agency what to do, how to do it, how much the doing should really cost, when the new campaign was needed and, by the way, the budget has just been cut and the schedule considerably shortened. Perhaps I exaggerate. But usually it's the result of people forgetting the simple truth of the relationship: everyone involved has a common and vested interest in the company's success.

Great Clients fully appreciate that. As far as they're concerned, people on either side of the table who don't understand this shouldn't be involved with the advertising.

# *Great Clients listen

Great Clients ask their agency important and relevant questions, the answers to which inform, clarify, enlighten. They ask questions to learn, not to challenge.

Great Clients know that if they don't ask questions and listen to the answers, they're shortchanging themselves and their company. After all, they expect that their agency will have the answers to their questions about marketing, sales, media, production, creative and so on.

On another level, listening is an indication of the agency's respect for the client. The obverse is also true.

Several years ago, a partner asked if I would attend an after-hours meeting with a start-up client who had just hired a new Marketing guy. Of course I attended the meeting. While my partner was giving the new guy a brief rundown of the agency and our capabilities, the guy took two phone calls and had two loud conversations. Rude. At the third call, I simply said, "Hang up!" He hung up, and then I explained how little interest he had displayed in what my partner was saying. I also explained that I wasn't going to waste my time listening to his conversations. The result? The fellow turned off his phone and paid attention until the meeting was over.

Great Clients know their business, their company and, to a certain extent, the people in their market. What they don't know is what an agency knows about their business—until they listen to them.

# *Great Clients don't expect free work

Great Clients know it's fairly easy to take advantage of their agency. But they don't. Call it manners, professionalism or just plain respect. (Most likely it's all of those.)

Typically an agency will go out of its way to accommodate a client. Agency people are hardly ever going to deny a client's request for work even when the task is really outside the boundaries of their contract, letter of engagement, handshake, etc. I'm talking about program ads for charity events, employee farewell parties, a son's birthday, employee contests, tee signs for a wife's golf tournament . . . you name it, the list is endless. Whatever it is, I've been asked to do this kind of work often enough to make a point of it here.

For example: I had a staff guy tell me that the Chairman wanted a full-page ad for his golf club's tournament program but didn't have the budget for it. That's OK. But in this case I had a hunch that the Chairman had not asked to have work done at no cost. I suspected that the ad was seen by a lower-level person as an opportunity to score points with the boss. Now, don't tell me I should start wearing a tinfoil beanie—I later had a brief conversation with the Chairman in which he told me he really liked the work, and to please send an invoice directly to him. That's when I had the opportunity to let him know we were pleased to have done it. Gratis.

The difference? They weren't extracting free work from me; the choice to take on the assignment was mine. I was happy to give the work away, because I didn't feel like they expected it from me.

# *Great Clients treat their agency fairly—usually

In the advertising business, the relationship between client and agency is often described as "adversarial." For good reason, I suppose. But I maintain that it doesn't have to be that way. Presumably an advertising agency provides specialized services that, typically, are outside the province of a client's business. Right?

Usually there will be some form of contract or letter of engagement detailing the services, costs and terms that client and agency have agreed upon as the basis of their professional relationship. In that agreement, the agency agrees to treat all client information (written or spoken) as proprietary and totally confidential for a period of time even after the agreement is terminated. Sounds fair to me.

In most agency/client agreements, there's also a clause stipulating that the agency will not look for, meet, talk with or accept work from any other company likely to be in competition with the client. This is where fairness is set aside. This is a one-way clause.

Just about every client I've worked with has balked at the idea of agreeing to a similar clause protecting the agency from getting screwed over. Put succinctly, clients have no problem talking or meeting with other agencies. Clients have no problem bringing another agency in to work on a project of some sort. Clients can secretly conduct a search for a new agency without telling their agency until they've selected one.

But if the client is protected by an exclusivity clause in their agreement, then the agency should have the same exclusivity clause at work for them. After all, shouldn't an agreement between two parties work for each party?

# *Great Clients don't set goals that can't be met

They give the agency a chance to review and discuss goals before taking on an assignment. If the goals are not realistic, the agency should say so, prove their point and offer goals that are achievable.

I once had a small auto insurance client that decided to start advertising in a metro area where they were steadily losing business. They had never, NEVER, advertised to their potential customers. Their reputation was a bit less than 100 percent, their rates were not always the lowest, their service was acknowledged to be slow. They offered no real compelling reasons to buy. And, if that weren't enough, their competition was well established, and trusted, in the marketplace.

Their goal for the first year? They wanted fifteen thousand new customers.

I talked with the client. I counseled that, in their situation, a few months of advertising should be devoted to building overall "awareness" and "perception," influencing how they wanted the market to see them. "First, you have to build awareness—get out there and make friends with your market!" I advised.

I talked with the group responsible for the media planning and buying. They agreed. We developed a campaign. We pitched it, they bought it for a ninety-day run and then they'd re-evaluate. We produced several good spots despite a low budget. The media group did its chart-after-chart thing. I'll spare you the details about how many spots we edited from the :30 and :60 originals. At the end, they had an astonishing number of spots, ready to air, at a ridiculously low cost per spot.

The day after the campaign broke, they called to tell me they'd not sold a single policy yet. The CEO was pissed. My group and I were doomed. I knew it. Soon enough, a consultant was brought in, and the media group was attacked and summarily dismissed. My inside contact advised me that the consultant was coming after me next.

Having fought and won some/lost some of those battles, I simply said, "I'm gone!" If clients can't bring realistic expectations to the table, there's no sense in sticking around.

# *Great Clients know that great creative doesn't come off an assembly line

Back in the sixties, some of the hottest agencies on "Madison Avenue" were tucked away in small hotel suites overlooking Third Avenue in Manhattan.

These were the agencies full of young men and women who approached their profession with a high heart, Ping-Pong tables, dartboards, jukeboxes and old barber chairs. Their creativity overflowed, and even the stolid, staid agencies started to set up Creative Departments that were cool 'n' hip.

It was also a time when Copywriters and Art Directors worked as a team. A team that shared an office. At BBDO/NY, the Creative Department occupied the eleventh floor at 383 Madison Avenue. Cubicles and offices were decorated by the occupant. All sorts of individual styles, memorabilia, dartboards, couches, overstuffed chairs, posters. It was exciting. From time to time you might even get a whiff of... a thought prompter.

One day I was asked to take a prospective client on a tour of the Creative Department. So I did. As we wandered through the entire department, the prospect remained fairly quiet, just the odd question every now and then. As we neared the end of our tour, we walked by a Copywriter's office. The Copywriter was at his desk, pounding away on his typewriter. The prospect made a comment, something like: "Good to see at least one guy is working."

We stopped for a moment. I explained: "Well, I guess you'd call it working, but for him it isn't work. His work is done. Now he's writing copy. The hard part of this job is finding a concept, an idea that works—a concept that can be turned into an exciting, compelling ad or commercial. Once that idea is found, discussed and evaluated, the copywriting is easy. His Art Director partner has already begun working on visuals and layouts."

Nothing has changed in the years since that day at BBDO/NY. Nothing important. Sure, typewriters and markers have been replaced with computers, tablets, styluses and all kinds of software that contribute to and help maximize the talents using them. The flow of information that can easily expand their knowledge base—and therefore their thinking—is amazing. But the challenges facing today's Copywriters and Art Directors remain the same. And a great concept is still a great concept.

Great Clients don't just recognize and value the creative side of the business; they understand the intense work that goes into producing great creative work—and they do everything they can to help create conditions for that work to emerge.

# *Great Clients see advertising costs as an investment, not an expense

I'd bet that virtually everyone in business recognizes the value of advertising. But then those very same people will immediately slide advertising onto a ledger column labeled "Expense."

Great Clients understand that an advertising agency and what it does is really an investment in their business. An investment not unlike the purchase of capital equipment, the hiring of someone with specialized skills, the development of a decent website, or the preparation of an instruction manual, to say nothing of making a brand well known and trusted in a marketplace.

No matter what the business is, no matter what it is a client wants to accomplish (unless the client wants to keep it all on the q.t.), advertising will play an important role in their success.

This is not to say that advertising budgets should be infinite. Like any investment, smart advertising requires a fair amount of homework so that resources can be deployed where they're most effective. If you know who they are and how your business or products can fit into their lives, how best to reach them and what you're going to say, then you'll be confident of a return on every ad dollar you invest in a campaign, or even in a single ad. It's that simple. That smart.

# *Great Clients don't expect instant miracles

Advertising is really all about building and maintaining high levels of market awareness. Great Clients know their advertising has to help make a "friend" every time someone sees their ad. Put another way: awareness leads to a trial, which generates consumer satisfaction, which leads to brand loyalty, which results in word of mouth.

Advertising can help reach goals quickly. But overnight? Not likely. Great Clients know that effective campaigns, ones that build a valuable brand, require a commitment of time, energy, money and creativity. It takes time to develop and manage reasonable goals and expectations.

Properly planned, coordinated and implemented advertising can help you build your business. Increased market awareness can create a climate for sales, help launch new products, solidify competitive product market position, create and maintain a corporate image and convey information that will actually help the consumer make an informed buying decision.

Chances are the TV commercials or video spots you really respond to, the newspapers and magazines you check out, the radio spots that resonate with you, are advertising for a Great Client—by an agency that received everything it needed to do its job well.

# *Great Clients know how to handle media... sort of

Television. Radio. Newspapers. Billboards. Magazines. Bus and taxi signs. Commercials in movie theaters (ugh), cable TV shows, barn sides, skywriting, supermarket baskets and floors... if there's a way to put a message on or in it, it's "media."

To a Great Client, "media" means the specific vehicles that carry the Great Client's message into a marketplace where people are most likely to respond. It's all about fact-based information, objectively presented.

Sounds simple. But a solid media plan is complex enough that it requires a media team to properly bring together all the important elements: research, costs, schedules, and fact-based media selection.

Whether the media pros are on the agency's staff or part of a media services group, the executive assigned to the Great Client's account will function much like your agency's

Account Executive. The media team or group executive will confront the following:

· Media plan development (starts with research)
· Media plan implementation (buying; getting the best deal)
· Media traffic (the right ad gets to the right publication etc.)
· Media reporting (effectiveness; is the plan working?)
· Media analysis (what to do when a station or publication isn't working)

Great Clients understand that the requirements for getting more bang for the media buck can include a specialist for each of the tasks listed here. Again, whether it's a staff Media Director, an in-house Media Department, or the use of a media service that handles it all... it has to be handled.

Great Clients make sure they know what's going on with their media folks. The biggest budget in advertising is the budget for media. For that reason alone, Great Clients aren't going to work with a rookie... they want and need a top-flight professional who really knows what needs to be done.

# *Great Clients know the internet is a tool, not a shortcut

I have a question: how far back in time is "back in the day"? Now, days seem to be moving with the speed of summer lightning. There was a time when creatives ran the agency. It was a golden age, when talent rose to the top and great advertising raised the bar considerably higher than it had been. Clients paid us to work our magic, and they were delighted when we presented our work.

Then there came a change. Lawyers and bean counters moved in. It was all about the numbers, ROI and the bottom line. Advertising became big business. And for a while the two sides, the creative and the suits, quietly argued over who was in charge.

Computers, software, digital presentations: tech guys started another revolution quietly in the back room. They'd show up when called upon. Load this piece of software. "Why did my computer go down?" "Can you help us set up a conference call?" "How does this thing work?" They'd help, for sure, and then go back to their lair. A darkened place filled with computer screens, keyboards, parts of things.

Then, for some inexplicable reason, the tech guys started talking with the agency's creatives and Account Executives while they were fixing, helping and designing better systems for the agency's communications and the agency's business.

Suddenly the tech guys who kept our computers running were sitting at the table. They were chiming in on creative, making a case for online ROI and channeling serious dollars away from traditional media into online avenues. That's when the Great Clients realized something big was upon them. The internet had landed. Both Great Clients and agency folks recognized its power and possibilities. Tech had arrived.

WHEN THE INTERNET first showed up as a new way to advertise, it was just about the sole subject of any conversation about media. I mean, how could you overlook the huge numbers delivered by a small ad that looks like a classified ad? But people often wondered why the results varied dramatically between one client and another. Questions like that are both easy and difficult to answer.

Not too long ago, I joined a small group called Glyphix, headed up by a guy named Larry Cohen, who had cofounded it along with two other guys. They were pretty smart. They recognized that something called the "Internet" could be of immense value to marketing and advertising.

I can't say that my experience with Larry and his group was filled with laughs and that we ended up rolling in money. However, I did learn a great deal about the internet, website design and development, social media and the people that developed the internet as a marketing tool. And, in turn, they learned that technology was not the answer to every question. That you don't really need to understand all the tech-speak. What you do need to understand is the potential it offers and how that potential can be realized.

The way I see it, the internet is not a magic wand that reaches in and changes customers' minds. It provides a massive reach at a lower cost, but the desired audience and delivered message must still be considered and measured the way you would with publications, radio, television, outdoor or direct response.

Most successful advertising in media other than the internet is successful because it crashes through the mental barrier that readers and viewers build against an incessant advertising assault. If you don't really know your customer, your agency can't create a message that'll penetrate that boredom the human mind has created to defend itself against the torrent of messages.

Knowing the customer is knowing more than simply where they go when they're browsing or looking for something specific on the web. You need to know a great deal more than demographics and keystrokes. You need to know how they think; how they feel; how they regard their job; how they spend their time with their children, if they have any, and if not, why they don't have any. You have to understand what their values are. In short, the more you know about what makes your customer tick, the better your chances are to reach them. No matter what the medium is, no matter how much money you spend, if the people you think will buy your product or service or message don't respond, most likely it's usually the result of delivering the wrong message to the wrong consumer at the wrong time.

# *Great Clients take their online presence seriously

When thinking about how to get great advertising from an ad agency, Great Clients know that most agencies will provide a range of digital services that include website design, development, building and even hosting. Additionally, if online advertising is needed, they'll easily handle that too. Same with all that goes into a campaign using social media.

Great Clients love the "trackability" of online advertising. Big data creates a wealth of information that informs precisely how your ad dollars are performing—and so communication between you and your Account Executive is vital. The agency should be able to clearly demonstrate how your ad spending is driving traffic and business. If they can do that, you've got a good team. They will justify every dollar they spend with metrics showing ROI. It's your job to give them a little running room to start and then adjust the campaign and spend as needed. Let them tell you what goals they set for your campaign and the time to meet them. Then hold them to it. Great Clients love meeting goals.

In the past, companies could overcome an advertising mistake. A bad ad, a product failure, a poorly timed promotion, a botched product launch. Today, things live on and on and on online. They live online all over the world, and your ads are seen by people you never intended. For that reason, it's so important to manage your online efforts, be they websites, blogs, participation on other social media sites, etc. We've seen the power of Facebook and Twitter and other tools, and they are only going to get more powerful as literally billions more consumers join the online shopping arena. Controlling your message is critical.

Work with your agency to really understand how they are using technology to deliver the results you're looking for, but keep the big picture in mind. Your agency is in the communications business and building a relationship between you and your customers is what matters, no matter how it gets done.

# *Great Clients know and understand the power of social media

Like everyone else, Great Clients hear a lot about social media; everyone seems to be developing programs for it. What is really important is to understand what social media is good at, and how it can work for you.

Social media is you speaking out loud, potentially to millions of people. Your message should be delivered the way you'd deliver it in person. Advertising, marketing, merchandising, sales promotion, public relations—whatever it may be, it should be your voice that the folks in your market hear.

Don't spend the time and money developing a social media campaign unless you're prepared to give the developers the time and resources for them to become "you." Social media speaks to your best prospects and customers with your voice. Just like you wouldn't hire a stranger to go to a friend's cocktail party and represent you, you shouldn't do that online. Online, they are you as far as your customers are concerned.

Are you seizing the opportunity to build brand awareness, gather research, sell product, strengthen customer relationships, answer questions, test out new products or ideas, fight bad PR? What do you hope to accomplish? Your goals will drive the look, feel, style and tone of the effort.

# *Great Clients put careful thought into their websites

Pretty much every company needs a website, but not every website needs to sell products, sign people up to newsletters or provide a VR tour of a store. Before you tell your agency, "Go build me a site," decide what you're hoping to achieve. Establish your goals up front so the agency can design and code toward that. But you must be mindful to make sure that all decision makers are involved. Countless sites have been ready to launch and then suddenly the CEO or other top management folks decide it's time for a review. At that point, fixes are very expensive and time-consuming.

Give the folks who will be providing content for the site early access to the information they need. Get them to meet relevant staff early in the process so everyone knows what needs to be included in the site. Don't make them guess or decide later. There is no "later" in the digital world. Later is too late and too expensive.

Meet frequently throughout the design process. If you have input, provide it then, not later. Making changes during the design phase is way less costly than once coding is started. And remember this: once the site is launched, prepare to do it all again soon—the speed with which markets move online, most websites need a refresh every couple years to avoid looking stale.

# *Great Clients don't let "the guys in the field" impact their advertising

I grew up in this business hearing that the "guys in the field," the people actually out there selling the product, were the most important people of all. And after all my years, after all the projects I've worked on, after all the clients I've had a side-by-side relationship with, I have concluded that's malarkey.

The guys in the field are, indeed, important. The good ones know their product and how to sell it. But face-to-face selling is quite different than advertising. Considerably different. Far too often the people in the field have a point of view that's a bit narrow.

They think "sales" is really "marketing." They hardly ever understand or agree with the conclusions delivered by research, and think they know more. But they probably don't. Because advertising is not what they do. Yet somehow they're considered important and valuable resources for the agency. Resources.

Smart agency folks will want to meet the people "the guys" work with "in the field": the distributors and retailers, agents or brokers and so on, who buy, sell or even use the product. All of these people will help enlighten the agency folks as to what your business and, ultimately, your customers—the folks who will actually buy what you have to sell—are all about.

To involve field Sales people with concepts, storyboards or rough layouts, etc. is a waste of everyone's time. Oh ... and involving them in "focus groups" is foolish, too. (I hear the howling.)

# *Great Clients don't use employees as a focus group

Employees are human beings. They buy stuff. All kinds of stuff. They watch TV, listen to the radio, read magazines and newspapers and go online. They know what they see and they have opinions. But they work for you! You pay them to work for you. They want to be your friend. They want to help you make the company more successful.

Often, employee attitudes skew toward the negative in the broadest sense of the word. Most often they will be critical of the work they're being asked to evaluate. I'm also sure that some will offer new headlines, media ideas and so on. That's my experience.

Focus groups are best developed by professional research people. They will screen a great number of consumers to get the few that most accurately represent your target audience. The process is arduous. And, as you probably know, focus groups are not quantitative. They are qualitative... kinda.

The best takeaways will still be personal attitudes and opin-ions. That's the way it is. But in the end, the strangers viewing the storyboards or print ads will provide a significantly more objective and useful response than employees.

# *Great Clients believe everyone is a proofreader

Typos are nasty, annoying little things. Demoralizing. Costly. Irritating. A pain in the ass to everyone. A typo is also avoidable.

If a proper approval process for creative and production is in place, and everyone on both sides has signed off all along the development and production process, then a typo is a shared responsibility. Which means that the costs involved with correcting the mistake should be split fifty-fifty. However, far too often the client holds the agency solely responsible for typos, even when the client has signed off on the work.

Is there a time when the agency should pick up the entire cost of correcting a typo? Yes. For example: when the client has approved the work up to a point, and the agency releases the work without further final approvals, the agency has just screwed itself and really should assume total responsibility for any cost involved with the correction.

When the agency is given information that's not current or accurate, that's when the client should pick up the entire cost of correction.

# *Great Clients keep meetings as small as possible

Simple truth: whether your company is large, medium or small, everyone on the payroll is interested in the company's advertising. This is good ... and bad, when it comes to the development, execution and implementation of advertising.

Put politely, Great Clients don't see the need to have everyone at every meeting with the agency. The reasons for meetings with your agency are few: research, creative (including production), media or troubleshooting.

How many people need attend? Great Clients restrict meetings to the core people and maybe a couple directly involved with the advertising. If there are more than four slated to attend, Great Clients rethink the list. Same with the agency side of the table. Core agency guys are all decision makers or influencers; those who can't make and quickly implement a decision concerning advertising aren't needed in the room.

If others are required, they can and should participate on an as-needed basis—they come in, say what they have to say and then leave.

This may sound a little stringent, but I can't tell you how many meetings I've attended to present creative work and had the (figuratively speaking) guy from the phone center lecture me about locations, lenses and camera angles. Please.

# *Great Clients don't bring an entourage to a TV shoot, rough-cut or final edit

Great Clients understand that the folks actually doing the work to produce a video are professionals working against a deadline. Great Clients understand that their presence at a production changes the dynamics—the production people will make sure the client is kept abreast of everything each step of the way, which slows everything down.

When Great Clients show up on the set (they actually do), it's only for a cup of coffee and a few quiet minutes with the agency's senior creative team members. They're just stopping by to make sure all is well and moving as planned. That's it.

Some clients, however, show up with a bunch of people who are there to see how a commercial is made. Or "they could use a break from the usual office routine." Or "when I told my nephews..." A client bunch can't help asking questions, being in the way, tripping over cables, talking loudly, wisecracking and, worst of all, suggesting. They ask for extra takes and call for changes to the script at the last minute, all while workers—who are on the clock—stand by idle. At the very least it's distracting. Sometimes disruptive. Always a nuisance.

For a series of commercials for an insurance company, we hired an Oscar-winning director. We had planned for three cameras at different angles to shrink a schedule by several shooting days. I arrived on the set around eight AM, looking for a cup of coffee and a donut. Instead I got a session with the director, who was complaining about the CEO. He had showed up early and insisted on seeing how each camera framed the shot, then suggested that we put up a special video feed to a dark corner. I nixed that and went looking for the CEO. I told him that, while I appreciated his intent, we simply could not have a discussion about shot framing every time we started to shoot. At this point we were trusting the (highly qualified) director. He understood, but was sulky until the director joined us for lunch and they had a fine conversation. The next three and a half days went quite smoothly. The CEO popped in a few times, enjoyed a donut and coffee, then split. As it should be.

Great Clients know a production isn't a party or a break in the routine for their staff or employees. The costs involved are primarily based on time. Which demands efficiency along with editorial talent. All in all, it is an amazing process, but it's not a process that invites conversation. And editing facilities are at work non-stop! Production is not exactly a nine-to-five job. This holds true for photography shoots, radio spot production—for whatever needs producing.

# *Great Clients don't manipulate the agency to get what they want

Here's a scenario for you: Creative work was being developed. An appropriate timetable was prepared and approved. The agency was beehive busy. Then a client person appeared and said, "Ms. Big wants the work completed and she wants to see it ASAP... like day after tomorrow." It's like a threat.

Now, here's the response most often expressed by the Art Directors and Copywriters doing the work: "Bullshit!" Indeed it is.

As an agency Creative Director, the question I'd ask is: "How come Ms. Big didn't call me or the AE directly?" *Stutter stutter* and *stammer* is the answer I'd get. That's the tip-off that Ms. Big probably asked how the project was moving along or, at the very worst, if it might be possible to see a preview of what the agency was doing.

The problem here is that someone on the client side is working an agenda while the agency works their butts off.

Deadlines can be adjusted; schedules can be reset. But far too often, Mr. Little will use Ms. Big's name to hammer the agency. Once the agency caves, it becomes a client's habit, and that's not a good thing for client or agency. It destroys agency morale and client credibility, both things that will, if left untarnished, drive the agency to push for better and better work.

# *Great Clients analyze failures before pointing fingers

If a campaign fails, some clients fire the agency and start looking for a new one. Sometimes they fire the internal marketing and/or advertising staff. They never fire themselves, however. Clients like this will pretty much do whatever it takes to avoid even partial responsibility, and so will never understand the mistakes that led to the failure.

A very wise advertising man once told me that vast amounts of advertising fail NOT because the advertising was lousy. They fail because no one took the time to find out if the consumer had any real interest in the product or service being offered. He's right. (Believe it or not, I've had a few clients refuse to spend on research!)

The vast majority of campaigns that fail do so because the folks you were trying to reach simply weren't given a compelling reason to respond, because no one took the time and effort to truly understand the customer and how—or if—the product fit into their lives.

If a campaign fails, revisit all the steps from the initial brief through creative execution to the media plan and eventual buy. Then look at the research the campaign was built upon. That's where the answer will be. And as you revisit each element, ask yourself, "What does this element do to help me understand and talk to the customer?"

Time-consuming, sure. But not rocket science.

# *Great Clients share responsibility for bad advertising

Frankly, if your agency isn't giving you work that you can willingly, happily approve most of the time, it may very well be that they may not "get it." Before you consider beginning the hunt for a new agency, though, consider the possibility that *you* don't get it. Or you're not giving it. (Uh oh.)

When a Great Client hears that "the agency just doesn't get it!" they stop and think carefully about:

· What the agency has a vested interest in
· What the agency's goals are if they know them
(if they don't know, they ask)
· The agency itself—its other clients, its reputation, etc.
· The way the agency responds to requests

If the agency comes out with positive marks, chances are it is giving you work that it believes will influence Jane and Joe Customer but not necessarily you or your staff. But the agency also must convince you that the work they bring you has a chance of succeeding in the marketplace. If you feel the end product isn't up to snuff, but the relationship is otherwise successful, it's time to look inward. Think about your people who are working with the agency. How do they regard and relate to the agency? If the boss has relegated the responsibility for making sure the agency "gets it" to staff, are those people working on their own agendas? But let's suppose for the moment that a change in agency is in order. (It actually happens! Even to Great Clients.) Now what?

# 5.

# How Great Clients Find the Right Agency*

THE MOST EFFECTIVE WAY to find the right agency begins with a single question: Why? Great Clients think long and hard about the answer.

If Great Clients have an agency and the advertising isn't working, they talk with their agency about concerns. Together, client and agency determine whether or not the problems can be resolved. If they can't, that's enough "why."

If you don't have an agency, the question applies equally. Make sure that bringing an agency on board will really help meet or exceed your stated objectives.

Not wanting to waste time, clients might contact an agency search firm. Working with a search firm will result in a long list, a short list, several presentations of agency credentials and, finally, several presentations (with too many people in them) of creative approaches to how each agency might help you meet goals. Zzzzzzzzzzzzzzzzzzzzz.

Great Clients figure if they can tell an agency search firm what's needed, they can easily conduct their own search.

# *Great Clients simplify the search

Advertising agencies share many of the basic problems confronting their clients, most of which are caused by people. All people have opinions, attitudes, feelings and knowledge (to one degree or another). People create politics and "situations."

Great Clients know this. They recognize that creating advertising inevitably invites subjectivity. That's why they try to keep as few people as possible involved with the selection of an agency and the development of advertising. And those are people chosen very carefully.

One lovely spring day, I decided to leave my office early, hop on my motorcycle and take a nice long ride through the San Gabriel Mountains. I went home, put on my gear, hopped on the bike, fired it up and rode slowly around the corner of the driveway and onto the hood of a brand-new Buick. I looked through the windshield at the face of a truly terrified driver. My new neighbor.

Afterwards, while my victim and I were having a glass of wine and swapping insurance information, he told me that he'd just finished a meeting with an advertising agency that was after his account. It was one of several boring meetings he'd had in his search for an agency. The conversation changed. I gave him my business card, chatted about my agency, showed him some of our work, and thirty minutes later I had a new client and he had a new agency.

He turned out to be a Great Client, and our working and social relationship continued for years. To be clear, vehicle accidents are not a great way to find an agency. But there are points to be made:

· A typical search involves several long, boring
meetings with agencies.
· My "victim" knew what he was looking for and
was ready to respond quickly when he found it.
· An informal conversation is a better way to find out
if the people you're talking with can get the job done.

While finding the right agency does require some thought, it doesn't have to become an endless process of meetings involving more and more people. Like just about everything else in the advertising business, the more people involved, the harder it becomes to make a decision, let alone the right decision.

# *Great Clients have smart meetings

Agencies abound. If you Google "advertising agencies" in your area, you'll find plenty to choose from. Spend a bit of time visiting websites. You'll find out who these people and their clients are. Most likely, you'll get to see a bunch of creative work that demonstrates how they solved problems. Note the ones that appeal and that feel right to you.

Then call them, talk with a senior management type and arrange to have lunch. Keep it small, informal and confidential. And make sure the Creative Director is brought along! Tell them about your company and what your expectations are. Ask them if they think they can help you meet goals. Be aware of this: they'll probably want to know what your budget is. At this point, I think, it's a bit early to talk about budgets. If you take them beyond this lunch, they'll have a chance to help you develop an appropriate number.

For the moment, I'm going to assume that you're the boss of your company, the Mr. or Ms. Big. So I'm going to suggest that all this lunchtime activity should be confidential until you announce that the company will be taking presentations from several advertising agencies. I'm suggesting this because if word gets out, you'll be inundated by agencies looking to make a pitch. Makes internal crowd control easier too!

This first meeting should be an easy, informal business lunch. The objective is to get a fix on three important things: their ability to think and their approach to advertising/creative; how effective they've been; whether they are people you'd like to know better.

SMART THINKING: "Thinking" is everything. Is your thinking compatible with the thinking of the agency and its top creative person? Ask about their philosophy, what their weak points are, about the scope of their people. Get deep. Ask what it takes to get great advertising. If you sense you're just getting standard agency answers, pass.

RESULTS: Ask them to give you a sense of how successful they've been for their clients on a scale of one to ten. Is there a result that they are most pleased with? Find out if they're capable of working in all media. Ask them about developing stuff like brochures. What campaign are they most proud of, and why?

CHEMISTRY: Sleeves-rolled-up communication is critical. This is what gets you, your people and the agency over the bumps, the long hours, the mistakes. Without "chemistry," communication will be tiresome, questionable and short lived. If an agency is boring, pass.

If you get back to your office feeling really good about the folks you've just met with, put them on your list. How many agencies you contact, how many lunches you have, depends on your availability and interest. If you can end up with three that you want to know more about, you've done a fine job. Those three agencies will be looking forward to making a presentation to you and those few people that'll be working directly with the agency.

# *Great Clients respect the pitch process

The decision to look for an agency has been made. Several really sharp agencies have been met with. The hunt is almost over. Three have been chosen to make a pitch for the account. What's next?

"Pitch Day" is next. The day when the agencies you've chosen get to show you just how good they are and convince you that you really need them working for you right away! Pitches often include a lot of razzle-dazzle. Yet take away the showmanship, presenting skills and quality of the charts they created, and what remains should be compelling reasons to buy them and their services.

Agencies live for new business presentations. They find preparing for a pitch to a possible client exciting. They know they're on a tight schedule, they know they'll be working long days and even nights. They know they're in a competition, and despite the groans and sniveling, they're having a good time!

Further, preparing and making a new business presentation consumes gobs of planning time, creative energy and money. In short, the agency is gambling that they'll win the competition. And whether the account is big or small, the competition is fierce. Understanding this, Great Clients plan on giving the agencies a fair amount of time to prepare.

Every new business presentation I've been involved with had a client-driven agenda. It was fairly simple: each participating agency had the same amount of time (sixty to ninety minutes) allotted for presentation of credentials, how the agency planned to handle the account, the agency's approach to media and/or research. The creative work (i.e., TV storyboards, print ads, logo designs, letterheads, etc.) concludes the presentation. Typically a Great Client will allow some time for questions after the agency has made its pitch, although, in practice, clients will ask questions as the agency presents.

That's a lot of ground to cover. If an agency can't meet this requirement, a Great Client will wonder about the agency's ability to schedule properly and meet deadlines. And because preparing for a new business presentation is costly on several levels, Great Clients may offer each participating agency a payment that will help defray the agency's costs. Doesn't have to be a lot, but it clearly defines the kind of client you are and are likely to be.

The same three elements described earlier (when you had a first lunch with possible candidates) will work at a different level during presentations. In sixty minutes (plus time allowed for questions), you should answer some simple questions that will lead you to the agency that's right for you and your company.

### SMART THINKING

· Is the creative focused and compelling?
· Was the attitude of the creative work consistent with the company's position?
· What, if anything, surprised you?

### CHEMISTRY

· Did the agency people involved gain your respect?
· Were your questions answered properly and directly?
· Can you imagine spending time with them in meetings, in an edit bay, in a photographer's studio?

### RESULTS

· Did the agency exceed your budget, meet it squarely or come in for less?
· Does the media plan offered deliver enough "bang"?
· If they pitched a larger budget, did they justify the bigger number?
· If they came in under, did they explain why?

If this sounds pretty straightforward, that's because Great Clients keep it that way. Not-so-great clients will throw in last-minute schedule adjustments, changing what the agency should be presenting, adding more agencies to review, asking for additional work without changing the agreed-upon date of the presentation and so on. Some may even want a sneak preview of the work being done. That's nasty, disruptive stuff.

As an aside, personally I didn't like to prepare new business presentations that were purely speculative. I told prospective clients that I had a problem with giving away what our clients paid for. I usually offered to estimate and bill for the real costs. If we were awarded the account, the amount of the invoice would be credited to their account with us. If not, the work we did would become the client's property. Seemed fair to me. Some people think it's crazy. I still think it's smart. When I suggested the above to one prospective client, they refused on the basis that our presentation should be seen as putting "some skin in the game." They stayed prospective clients.

In most cases, Great Clients will want a sense of how an agency's creative folks would respond to the challenge. (More often than not, the agency that pulls out all the stops to convince you is the one that will get it ) From start to finish, preparing a really good presentation will be time-consuming and very expensive.

If you don't pay even a token amount, the agency doesn't have to leave the work with you. Should you agree to pay the agency, the work belongs to you. Time for a small tale . . .

At one point, I had a very unlikable but smart client. His son was the second-in-command. Somewhat arrogant, but smart. He left the company to take a senior position with a high-tech company in another city. Within a few months, I was called and arranged to consult with him for a period of time. He was very unhappy because he couldn't find the right agency. On my first visit to his offices, I discovered that the apple really doesn't fall far from the tree. In just a short period of time, he had managed to gain a reputation within the ad community for being a real pain in the behind. Agencies simply weren't interested in working with him. So I called a few of the major agencies in that city. We chatted, and they said they'd "think it over"... and would I stay in the picture. I said yes. A few days later, the three agencies agreed to make a pitch. That's when I told them they'd receive a payment of $5,000. In short, the pitches were great, the agencies were more than pleased with the client's thoughtfulness, and his reputation was fully restored. And the agency that won the pitches had a client for some time.

When you've seen the pitches, the only thing left to do is pick the agency. It's that simple, that efficient and that productive. It's simple because you've limited the number of your people involved to two or three. Small groups like this will discuss things more fully and then make a decision. Larger groups tend to need a consensus and a date when a decision is needed by.

If you still can't decide after meeting with the agencies and seeing their presentations, well, I submit that the problem lies within you. But don't despair...

Pick the agency you and your core people believe is best. Then tell the agency you want to be engaged before you get married. Make it a three-month engagement. They'll get paid for these months. If everything works out for the first three months, then you'll be happy to sign a contract with the agency. Simple, reasonable and smart.

# Conclusion:
# It's a People Thing

Like all clients, Great Clients are people. They make all kinds of decisions every day. Decisions about their personal life. Decisions about their business life. About the kind of people they want to share their workday with. But they view things from a slightly different perspective than most clients. They see things in terms of relationships. Often they go to great lengths to establish and maintain relationships with interesting, intelligent, resourceful and thoughtful men and women. Personal or business, their approach is, essentially, the same.

In my time, I've worked with Great Clients and those considerably less than that. Advertising, especially advertising, is a service business. And so I've worked with clients that have made me grit my teeth before every meeting. And I've worked with clients who put as much into our relationship as I did. Neither of us wanted to disappoint the other.

Not every Great Client does everything discussed here. However, the point of it all is that Great Clients want their advertising agency to be an integral part of their management team; the part of a team whose work impacts virtually everything the client's company does. These clients are professionals and, as such, they expect a high level of professionalism from their agency in return. Not only that, their advertising is way better than most. That's what it's all about.

# Acknowledgements

A writer has an idea. (It's not a book.) Then the writer translates that idea into words on a page. (It's still not a book.) Sometimes the writer shoves his pages into a desk drawer. (Definitely not a book.) But every now and then the writer stumbles onto a publishing company (Figure 1), and the publisher himself (Chris Labonté) suggests there may be a book in this manuscript. (It's still not a book.) And so a team of people like Michael Leyne, Breanne MacDonald, Richard Nadeau, Peter Norman, Mark Redmayne, Lara Smith, and Jessica Sullivan handle all the tasks that result in a real book. This book. Amazing.

Many thanks to all the clients that made every day an adventure: American Standard, Armstrong Cork Company, Appliance Industries, Bausch & Lomb, Burndy Corp., Campbell Soup, Chevron Oil, Coldwell Banker Commercial, Dri Mark Products, DuPont, Gallo Winery, Hammermill Paper, Hoffman Bros. ("Hoffy"), Independence Bank, Lance Campers, Los Angeles Kings, Mattel, Packard Bell, Practical Peripherals, Remington Sporting Firearms, Safeway Stores, Superior Industries, *The New York Times*, Timken, True Temper Corp., and Warner Bros. Consumer Products ... and apologies to those I may not have listed here.

DAVID ULLMAN worked for "a very long time" in the creative trenches of advertising agencies in New York and Los Angeles, from Madison Avenue heavyweights, to the successful agency he co-founded, to a boutique agency that was ahead of its time in focusing on the internet as a marketing and advertising tool. He's worked in all media for big, medium, and small clients. Along the way he won a few awards and made a bunch of friends. He now lives in Victoria, B.C.